OEDIPAL HERO

OEDIPAL HERO

The Hidden Side of Glory

by Peter Fritz Walter

Published by Sirius-C Media Galaxy LLC

113 Barksdale Professional Center, Newark, Delaware, USA

Set in Avenir Light and Trajan Pro

Designed by Peter Fritz Walter

ISBN 978-1-981931-70-5

Publishing Categories
Psychology / Social Psychology

Publisher Contact Information
publisher@sirius-c-publishing.com
http://sirius-c-publishing.com

Author Contact Information
pfw@peterfritzwalter.com

About Dr. Peter Fritz Walter
http://peterfritzwalter.com

Parallel to an international law career in Germany, Switzerland and the United States, Dr. Peter Fritz Walter (Pierre) focused upon fine art, cookery, astrology, musical performance, social sciences and humanities.

He started writing essays as an adolescent and received a high school award for creative writing and editorial work for the school magazine.

After finalizing his law diplomas, he graduated with an LL.M. in European Integration at Saarland University, Germany, and with a Doctor of Law title from University of Geneva, Switzerland, in 1987.

He then took courses in psychology at the University of Geneva and interviewed a number of psychotherapists in Lausanne and Geneva, Switzerland. His interest was intensified through a hypnotherapy with an Ericksonian American hypnotherapist in Lausanne. This led him to the recovery and healing of his inner child.

In 1986, he met the late French psychotherapist and child psychoanalyst Françoise Dolto (1908-1988) in Paris and interviewed her. A long correspondence followed up to their encounter which was considered by the curators of the Dolto Trust interesting enough to be published in a book alongside all of Dolto's other letter exchanges by Gallimard Publishers in Paris, in 2005.

After a second career as a corporate trainer and personal coach, Pierre retired as a full-time writer, philosopher and consultant.

His nonfiction books emphasize a systemic, holistic, cross-cultural and interdisciplinary perspective, while his fiction works and short stories focus upon education, philosophy, perennial wisdom, and the poetic formulation of an integrative worldview.

Pierre is a German-French bilingual native speaker and writes English as his 4th language after German, Latin and French. He also reads source literature for his research works in Spanish, Italian, Portuguese, and Dutch. In addition, Pierre has notions of Thai, Khmer, Chinese and Japanese.

All of Pierre's books are hand-crafted and self-published, designed by the author. Pierre publishes via his Delaware company, Sirius-C Media Galaxy LLC, and under the imprints of IPUBLICA and SCM (Sirius-C Media).

Pierre's Amazon Author Page

http://www.amazon.com/Peter-Fritz-Walter/e/B00M2QN4SU

Pierre's Blog

https://medium.com/@pierrefwalter

CONTENTS

INTRODUCTION

An Uninvestigated Psychiatric Problem

Since long I carry with me the idea to write about what I perceive is a barely investigated behavior pattern to be found among those raised since the baby boom in the 1970s and 80s, and for the most part without breastfeeding. And they have suffered from tactile and sensual deprivation in many other forms as well, as that generation was growing under the spell of a really devilish pediatrics that in its life-denying ignorance arrogantly kept parents from touching their children.

Co-sleeping of parents and children, originally an activity that forms part of the natural continuum, was declared a crime, and assumed to be just another form of covert incest they had discovered as the newest cry in fashionable popular psychology.

—See the important study by Jean Liedloff, The Continuum Concept (1977/1986) that was written in that same era of the 1970s, and that clearly marks the turning point in that it shows with much anthropological evidence that Western culture was clearly steering into an abyss with their modern touch-denying childrearing paradigm.

Parents caressing their children were blamed as perversely sensuous and weak, as fondling and caressing was connoted with 'spoiling the child.'

Sexual permissiveness, while often declared as *in* for educated people, turned out to be a media bluff, as researchers clearly unveiled.

—See John P. Alston & Francis Tucker, The Myth of Sexual Permissiveness (1973).

This alienated child-rearing paradigm, *Made in USA*, as so much of the same that is now exported worldwide, was assiduously absorbed and cloned by parents in Britain, Australia, Germany and France, and to a lesser extent in Italy, Spain or Greece. In fact, Mediterranean culture was always strongly in favor of sensuality in the parent-child relation, and generally is much more erotically intelligent as any country from the Anglo-Saxon world with their debilitating history of life-and-love-denying Puritanism.

Even today, while most of Spockian assumptions have been found to betray the very core of healthy nutrient childcare, Dr. Spock's manual is still sold.

—See for example, Dr. Spock's Baby and Childcare (2004).

And, interesting coincidence, the Dr. Spock who wrote it has not little in common with the character of the same name in *Star Wars*. Both emphasize the priority and supremacy of the intellect, and belittle, if not deny, the innate intelligence of our emotions. The star war plot explains that the Vulcans have assessed themselves as being 'too emotional,' which had created strife and turmoil in their relationships and political dealings.

As a result and as it were as a remedy for their high emotionality, they did away with emotions as much as they could, developing something like a *Spartan* attitude or lifestyle, which puts rationality first, as something like a supreme value, and which assures that in all their shortcomings, the intellect always got the overhand over their emotions. Facial expression, way of addressing others, verbal communication and body language of Spock expresses this attitude very concisely. His diction is short and crisp, his remarks to the point, his empathy one of polite and calculated aloofness, his critique biting and always brilliant.

He is able to demonstrate to everybody around that he's intellectually superior, by nature, or by birth, simply because he's a Vulcan. But this attitude, we know it very well among us other humans! And this is one of the attitudes of the *Oedipal Hero* I am going to talk about in this chapter, because attitudes betray. Attitudes are sign posts, not just the little critter in our daily relationships.

I do not say that *Star Wars* is a particularly Oedipal kind of production. In *Star Wars*, the *Oedipal Hero* is given a three-fold expression, part being incarnated by Captain Kirk, part by Spock and last part, the hero's shadow, by Darth Vader.

But this book is not about Star Wars, and this was just an example. This book is not about movies either, but about psychology. I would say it's the psychology of psychoanalysis, the truth about this tragic character called Oedipus that Sigmund Freud dug out from the Greek's huge reservoir of mythology for explaining the child's psychosexual development.

To put things in straight terms, and to give an idea what this rather queer book about, let me say this. I have not just vague, but clear-cut objections against Freud's theory and have put them up in eight points.

—See Peter Fritz Walter, Normative Psychoanalysis: How the Oedipal Dogma Shapes Consumer Culture (Scholarly Articles, Vol. 14), 2015/2017.

I will not repeat this critique here because this is not what the present study is about. I go beyond Freud, and not only. More importantly, I go beyond Oedipus.

Oedipus was not the starting point of the human race. He was rather the starting point of the *decline* of the human race. I will show in this book that the man Oedipus is not what is really interesting about him. He was pretty much a victim of circumstances. So what actually counts in Sophocles' tragedy is not Oedipus, but the circumstances that pushed him around like a boat in heavy sea.

All tragedies have in common that the good will of the hero did not positively affect his destiny—even to the contrary. And here is a leitmotiv of this study: it's rather the hero's too-goodness, as it were, that throws him in the abyss, that makes him a prey of bad forces.

This goodness is false, it's the narcissistic shell that hides the shadow. Second, when we investigate those circumstances that made out of Oedipus' life an endless series of twists and turns, and ended him up in an impasse, we see that there is something like a curse upon him, or his family.

His father got the strangest oracle one can ever think of: he will be killed by his own son. The horrified man set the baby out on a mountain, for who wants to have it may take it. And a shepherd had a good soul: he said why others, and not me, and took the baby, and through his good deed, the baby landed in the arms of a king's family, while himself being from royal origin.

The terrible fate is here, and that's one vision of it, that by the very will of Oedipus' father, King Laius, to avoid the fatal prediction, he was setting all in place to fulfill it. The other vision of it would say: anyway, if he had kept the boy, the prediction would have been fulfilled as well. Speculation does not help. We do not know. It was as it was. He wanted to avoid the worst and abandoned the baby. That would be an interesting topic for a poll, I guess, to see how many people would act like him, and how many would take a different action —and which action?

A psychological view of the story penetrates deeper into the mystery of *karma*. To put it squarely: nobody gets fatal predictions who has a good karma.

So who had the bad karma? First of all, the father. Here is the key of the story. We have a father and a son. Everybody says the son is the bad guy but the curse was coming upon Oedipus through his father.

No curse comes from nothing, karma is *cause and effect*. And here we are at the very core of the character that I came to call *Oedipal Hero*. He is the savior of his parents in saving them, consciously or not, from their family curse, their *Verzauberung*, their narcissism, their undealt life issues, and their bad karma. And his very mission to save them is his— misunderstood— heroism, what makes him a *false hero*.

Well, in this moment it should ring in the reader's ears, as it should appear obvious from this point of my explanations that what the Oedipal trap in fact leads to is *narcissism*, but I see that differently than mainstream psychiatry. The difference consists in the fact that I see an entanglement, a *missing link* between the tragedies of both Oedipus and Narcissus that I have never seen mentioned in any psychology or psychiatry treatise, nor in any work on mythology. Generally, the two stories are explained as standing for different psychological complexities. This is of course generally true, but that does not exclude that they can be seen together as well.

The astonishing thing is that when you do this, as I did it for the first time back in 1992, when I wrote my first sketch on this problem, you will see not just one door, but a whole series of doors opening in front of your eyes, and you will discover the whole why-and-how our culture is so hopelessly entangled in parent-child codependence, widespread emotional abuse of children, a true denial of love, violence, self-alienation, narcissism and widespread, non-diagnosed, and more or less socially accepted *schizophrenia*.

And you will also begin to understand the true etiology of pedophilia, a problem that until now is not understood by Western psychiatry, while a certain acceptance has been established in the meantime for all paraphilias.

The fact that pedophilia is not understood makes it easy for political opportunism to gain the overhand and put up pedophiles as a new scapegoat group that is to be sacrificed for the sake of public order and other fake agendas that serve right-wing and outright fascist leaders to hide their *overall incompetence* and their pitiful spiritual ignorance to manage political affairs in a highly complex world.

This vacuum that we are facing right now is to be blamed on mainstream psychiatry that joined the right-wing and fascist forces since long in helping to condemn as a curse and condemnation a sexual orientation it has never understood because it ignores its etiology. The political consequence, then, is to demonstrate that the public is being misinformed, and perhaps intently so, in order to believe that pedophilia was a family curse, a genetic default, or another sort of mental debility.

All these assumptions have been voiced over time, but they are what they are, hypotheses. In addition, self-labeled pedophiles added on to the confusion by the very fact of their self-labeling. Their public and online campaigns for acceptance of childlove were not only hitting granite, but worsened their overall condition as a sexual minority worldwide; this is so because they steered public with the wrong strategy.

Instead of understanding that sexuality is not rigid and eternally determined, this small but influential group of pedophiles going public tried to gain social acceptance in a similar way as formerly the homosexuals, namely by affirming time and again they were born 'as such.' And that very argument of course turned against them in the long run, as it turned against the homosexuals, while the latter still go on to believe they had gained something like long-term social acceptance. In crisis situations and when polemics rise because the reigning strata need again a scapegoat for obfuscating their pitiful corruption and political incapacity, the homosexual cause will be torn up again, and anarchy and chaos will again break down the walls not of silence, but of their bars, shops, cafés and houses.

Contrary to both right-wing polemics and mainstream psychiatric ignorance, I have shown in other more specific publications that sexuality is by no means a rigid and fixated condition, and that once the functionality and the *flow nature* of the sexual energies is understood, all sexual attraction can be changed, however not by coercion, not by imposing a behavior standard on certain people, not by force. Not by violence. It can change by itself when the person begins to weigh other love options, and takes chances in other sexual avenues.

> —See Peter Fritz Walter, The Energy Nature of Human Emotions and Sexual Attraction: A Systemic Analysis of Emotional Identity in the Process of the Human Sexual Response, 2015/2017.

Sexuality is a matter of choice and predilection, and first of all of *emotional attraction* that by and by becomes sexualized. Hence, emotional choice primes before it ever becomes a subject of sexual reasoning. And here is where I deliberately contradict modern sexology that in its mechanistic Cartesianism is unable to grasp *the primacy of our emotions*, and the fact that sexual attraction follows emotional predilection, and not the other way around.

I have since long analyzed the public demonstration of pedophiles as the search for a *fake identity*, which is just another manifestation of narcissism, but it has to be seen that those who came up with these slogans are a tiny minority within a minority. Contrary to the standard assumption of mainstream psychiatry, not all pedophiles are narcissistically fixated, and not all pedophiles are rigid, exclusive and inflexible in their love choices. Those who are, and who have been at the forefront of the public discussion, are not representative. They have to be blamed with the same kind of ignorance as their opponents, putting up in their public forums notorious assumptions about as it were the 'phylogenetic' if not the 'biogenetic' etiology of pedophilia.

It is so easy to blame the fate of birth for all our misfortunes in life, and it is most often a denial of responsibility to accept one's destiny.

Destiny, contrary to folk wisdom, is not a predestined fate, but pure potentiality. Nobody is born a mathematician, a genius, a homosexual or a pedophile, in the same way as nobody is born a masturbator. There is potentiality for a certain pathway of self-realization, be it professionally, or in love. Those pedophiles who told their story to the public did this probably in an attempt to be taken for what they are, in a naive hope society would finally drop the debate and say 'Well after all, if they are so, and born like that, we should better accept them.'

Yet society does not reason that way. Nicolas Sarkozy and many other social policy makers are reasoning out ways to establish new euthanasia laws that in their fascist worldview would *end for all times* the problem of pedophilia in much the same way is Hitler's megalomanic idea of 'total war.'

Those narcissistic freaks who were at the forefront of the debate of pedophilia, as the self-chosen representatives for a community the contours of which can hardly be defined in scope and quantity, have served their own deficient egos, but they did a bad service to the cause of loving children erotically. They brought this cause down through their rigidity and their fear to be homeless, having chosen the haven of pedophilia addiction as their new home, as the hanger for their fragile identity, because they never really cared about their soul values and their spiritual belonging. This is true narcissism, this denial of soul, this denial of complexity, and here the pedophile propagandists and their opponents, the *Oedipal Heroes*, have much in common! And this is why, as a matter of holistic logic, they had to clash. Because, if they know it or not, they have much to share!

The truth? Not to be found on either side of the ring, but in its very center, halfway between the extremes.

The *Oedipal Hero* suffers from exactly the same hangup as the pedophile, with the only difference that they repress their pedophile desire and project it on others.

The way out is not pedophilia or anti-pedophilia, because it's the wrong question. The right question is to ask if the repression of children's emotional and sexual life is bringing anything positive to children, or if rather the absence of such repression brings the true benefit for children's healthy growth?

Both the *Oedipal Hero* and the *Propagandist Pedophile* are blind-eyed to see that the only tangible and provable etiology of both the Oedipal fixation and pedophilia is the emotional and tactile starving, and the sexual deprivation of children and adolescents, as it's rampant in postmodern industrial bourgeoisie since about the second half of the 17th century.

When the complexity of sexuality is understood, and once it's energetic nature is clearly seen, when its changeable and fluid nature eventually has been accepted, we are one step ahead. When the true etiology of pedophilia is defined within a larger systemic interdependence with other social factors, we are two steps ahead. When we see that we do not need any polemics about pedophilia, that we do not need to bother at all with this matter, nor with homosexuality or other paraphilias, we are at the point to recognize that what we have to tackle is the *education of our children*, the way we help them integrate their emotional and sexual energies, the way we look at them as complete beings, not dwarfs who are limited, because of lacking growth, to express their emotional and sexual feelings.

Then, as a matter of systemic logic, when we have changed the social and legal situation as a result of our insight in the importance of respecting children's integrity, and our responsibility to do away with all violence in relating to children, be it educational, then our culture as a whole will change. And the problems of homosexuality, pedophilia, sadism, masochism and what I know more sexual fixations will be no problems anymore.

I do not imply that these manifestations of the life energy will completely disappear, but a society that has eventually accepted the child, and the child within, will be able to accept *sexual diversity* as it accepts ethnic, racial and social diversity.

And as an advice to those who recognize themselves as being different from the sexual norm, I would like to say this:

ADDRESS TO PEDOPHILES

Do not absolutize your sexual attraction whatever it is like. It may change tomorrow as a matter of overall change of your life and love options, as a matter of personal growth, or as a matter of deliberate choice. When you absolutize and dogmatize your sexuality, you are on the same track as the Oedipal Hero who takes his Oedipal hangup, and the whole ridiculous macho behavior that results from it, as eternal and unchangeable. Fact is that we can change all in life, as life itself is unending change. Those who deny this fact are more often than not situated on the right wing of the political spectrum and their denial of complexity is just one element of their emotional distortion and mental debility. The cause of childlove is no cause, as love itself cannot be a cause. This is so because love cannot be defined. And what cannot be defined cannot be made a cause. Any cause of action for love will thus be the cause of action for a *concept of love* you have made up in your mind before you ever started out to be an activist for that cause. The real cause that is hidden behind the fake cause of childlove is the cause of the child. It's as simple as that, and in two senses of the word: in the sense of a cause for your own repressed inner child, who needs your empathetic inner parenting, and of the cause of the children all around you whose emotional and sexual needs are shunned by present society's many Oedipal Heroes who fight against the proverbial windmills instead of seeing the real causes. The cause of the child I am talking about is a cause that will not serve the Oedipal Hero in his or her eternal striving for glory nor your ego for sexual fulfillment with children, which may equally serve your personal glory. The cause of the child is paradoxical in that it helps the child to become an adult, that it serves the child to grow, and against both Oedipal culture's and your interest as a pedophile, to grow out of childhood as fast as possible.

It goes without saying that I will treat these subjects in this chapter, as in all of my books, in a scientific manner, avoiding polemics pro or con while I admit that I better understand and can better empathize with those who are arguing *pro life* and *pro desire* than those who argue *pro morality* as a doctrine to replace nature by culture.

From this natural bias, that is based not on belief or dogma, but on knowledge, I may argue in ways that provoke anger and revulsion in those who are eternally stuck in the league of moralism, of life hate, and of religious fundamentalism. Be it so.

THE COMPLETE OEDIPUS STORY

A Lesson in Mythology

What Freud did was to mutilate the Oedipus saga for it is originally imbedded in a greater epic cycle, the tragedy of the *House of Thebes*, as it is referred to in mythology. The myth must include, to be fully understood, at least one generation before Oedipus, and one generation after him. Without seeing the family curse, how can Oedipus' tragedy and suffering be understood? And if it's not understood, how can the tragedy and suffering of the consumer child in *Oedipal Culture* be understood?

The Oedipus saga is the account of a family curse. It is about what the ancient Greek called 'offending the gods,' what Christians, Jews and Muslims call *sin*, and what in modern language is called an abuse story.

The family curse aspect of the abuse was in this family especially pronounced in that it went over several generations. But the expression *family curse* is inept as it suggests something like an outside agent or a dubious notion of fate that triggers, like a Damocles sword, people's destruction. To believe this is an error. It can well be made out, when analyzing this family story, who the culprits were, and how what they did triggered a negative response.

In case of that family, it is true, the behavior of our heroes was particularly harsh and the response of the universe was equally harsh, and even cruel. We have to keep in mind that it is an extreme case, but it's a good moot court trial. It shows as it were the principle. Liz Greene and Juliet Sharman-Burke write in *The Mythic Journey (2000)*, p. 51:

> The mythic history of the House of Thebes is a dark one, and begins even before Oedipus himself. Sin follows sin in this family, worse than any television soap opera, and the line is plagued by the curses of various offended gods. The House of Thebes is the ultimate 'dysfunctional family.'

My hypothesis is that Freud chose the Oedipus saga as a metaphor for the psychosexual development of the child at the onset of the genital response because he knew or assumed that our culture is incestuous in its very roots, and abusive, especially in the parent-child relation. How else could a sane mind dig in human mythology to find the most abysmal story ever told about human vileness, and glue it on the back of every innocent little child? And here the word 'innocent' virtually rings in my ears—because it sounds false.

If ancient mythology is true, we are *not innocent*, not even as small children, as we bear, each of us, our individual and our family karma, if we want or not, as a matter of universal law. But I won't give a judgment here, I won't jump to any conclusion, and leave this question open.

Let us instead look at the details of the saga of Thebes and see what water we can draw from it for our question if Freud's theory of the Oedipus complex bears truth and can be validated, or if it has to be dismissed as a cultural projection upon human nature.

Liz Greene and Juliet Sharman-Burke write in *The Mythic Journey (2000)*:

> This tale is concerned with what the Greeks understood as the family curse—an offense against a god which is punished through successive generations.

In modern psychological terms, we might understand this as the passing down of unresolved family conflicts. What our parents have not dealt with, we may find ourselves facing, and these 'sins of the fathers' will in turn pass to our children if we do not deal with them. (Id., 51)

Now let us look at the facts first. Laius, the King of Thebes received from the oracle in Delphi a prediction he might be killed by his own son. The answer could have consoled him in a way because he was childless and it was exactly for that reason that he came to consult the oracle. So he could have reasoned, 'well, it was not meant to be, then.'

But what did he? He first cast out his wife Jocasta. As she did not know why her husband wanted to get rid of her, she managed to get him drunk and made love with the drunken man—and got pregnant, as she had intended it.

This sounds quite strange, as the couple had been childless before, but anyway, it appears the invisible threads of destiny were already at work. And Laius was anxious then, and as soon as the child was born, took the next chaotic step in *unknowingly fulfilling the oracle:* he took the baby to a mountain, pierced his feet with a nail and left him there, exposed to all dangers.

Coincidentally, the protector spirit of the Delphic oracle is Apollo, and the child-protecting gods were with the Greeks equally Apollo, and his sister Artemis, which is why they were infuriated, and it was this act that triggered the whole series of tragedies to come.

These gods then let a shepherd find the baby who named him *Oedipus* which in Greek means 'swollen foot.'

By another turn of destiny, the baby got in the arms of the Royal Family of Corinth where Oedipus grew up in good and equal standing.

One day, somehow anticipating his destiny, Oedipus went to Delphi to ask the oracle about his future, and got from Apollo the terrible oracle he would murder his father and marry his mother. In a chaotic streak of action that reminds of his father, Oedipus did not return to Corinth, determined to prove the god wrong. He took his adoptive parents for his true parents and thought that by simply not being around them any further, he could avoid the fate. Apollo however was infuriated about so much human willfulness and sheer arrogance, and the next turn of destiny was again a blunt fulfillment of the prediction.

As a strange turn of events, Oedipus happened to meet the chariot of King Laius, but he did not know it was his father. Laius told the young man to step off the road, Oedipus gave a rude reply, and the king let the chariot roll over Oedipus foot, thus opening the old wound. In a fury, Oedipus flung Laius on the road and drove the horses over him, thus murdering, unknowingly, his father. In addition, what was considered a particularly heavy crime in ancient Greece, he left the dead corpse to lie unburied in the dirt.

Here, the myth seems almost unbelievable. When we consider that Laius was a king, how could it be that he was attacked so easily by a youngster who happened to cross his way, without enjoying any protection from the part of the chariot driver and other staff?

Coincidentally, Laius had been on his way to Delphi again, to find appeasement for having abducted a young boy for sex, whereupon the gods had sent to Thebes an ugly monster, which settled at the city gate asking every passenger a riddle: 'What being, with only one voice, has sometimes two feet, sometimes three, sometimes four, and is weakest when it has the most?' Oedipus, who went to Thebes straight after the murder of his father, guessed the right answer and replied:

—Man, because he crawls on all fours as an infant, stands firmly on his two feet in youth, and leans upon a staff in his old age.

The monster vanished and Oedipus was made King of Thebes, and he married Jocasta, his own mother, without of course knowing what he was doing.

But his glory did not last as a blind seer arrived at the court and declared that King Oedipus was the murderer of Laius. Nobody believed him but the Queen of Corinth then spread the information about Oedipus' origins. Jocasta committed suicide, and Oedipus blinded himself and, pursued by the Furies, cursed his sons (and brothers) Eteocles and Polyneices, and went into exile.

And here we see the curse taking over the next generation. After many years of wandering about the world, guided by his daughter-sister Antigone, Oedipus died, but peace did not come to the House of Thebes. Both Eteocles and Polyneices died in the war that broke out over the succession to the Theban throne. And Antigone was sentenced to death because she had released her dying brother's spirit against the order of her father Creon. Polyneices' son attempted to regain the throne, but lost the battle and Thebes was sacked.

A Teaching Tale?

Authenticity Doubts

I honestly wonder if we can believe in the authenticity of this old myth?

There are at least three incidences where the plot is against common sense, when we consider the custom of the times it originates from. And independently of that context, the credibility of the tale is weakened by lacking probability. These incidences are:

—A patriarch who casts his wife out will not possibly invite her again for sharing a meal with her. How could Jocasta get her husband drunk if he did not revoke his repudiation and invited her to join him again? And if he did, her act of forcing him to copulate with her to get her pregnant when he was drunk is at least equal in low spirits to his harsh act of repudiating her. In ancient patriarchy, an act of repudiation did not need to be justified in any way. Every man had the right to cast his wife out at any moment. And of course, he equally had the right to take her again if he repudiated her in a hot temper. If the story says they were sharing a meal and wine was consumed, this means that he had taken her again, and thus the harsh act of repudiation was forgotten.

To construe an evil act out of the repudiation as such, as Liz Greene and Sharman-Burke do in saying he had to inform his wife about the reason of casting her out, is a typical trap-reasoning of modern psychologists, who interpret meaning *into* old myths, instead of taking meaning out of them.

—A royally bred and educated young man infuriated about a king's chariot, reacts rudely and then, because the chariot doesn't make way, gets hurt, and as a retaliation bluntly murders the king, tearing him down from his chariot like a street robber would do, and then mounts the horses to treat him in the dust? Wait a moment, this may fit in a Hollywood story, but it doesn't fit in that time. A king was not driving his own chariot, and he was not being driven in any kind of chariot, but a royal chariot, and he had a horseman, or several horsemen, for doing that, and there were a number of other people around who would have prevented the young man from tearing the king down in the gutter and then let the horses tread him in the ground.

—A king abducting and 'raping' a young boy? Wait a moment again, and look at what *boylove* means in ancient Greece, and what abduction means! And here, a look at the original text would be needed for Green and Sharman-Burke call 'rape' is again something that is most of the time interpreted into old myths.

I have demonstrated in my book 'Minotaur Unveiled' that the abduction of noble boys was prohibited by law in ancient Greece, but not the abduction of slave boys. Abduction was at that time a frequent means for having a fortnight of intercourse with a pubescent boy. This kind of abduction was not, as today, followed by murder. In the regular case it was followed by setting the youngster free after giving him a more or less important gift that depending on the social status of the lover could be a substantial remuneration. As a matter of fact, abduction was frequently in old patriarchy the foreplay of a marriage as well; this is true for both Jewish culture and ancient Greece and Rome. The only obligation a lover had when abducting a girl for sex was to marry her, or to pay a compensation to the father of the girl in case he did not. When the lover was a king, he certainly had the right to enjoy sex with young people, as this was the custom of the time, and here, his responsibility was conditioned to paying an indemnity to the boy or his family.

Without considering all these details, to construe out of Laius' boylove an offense against the gods, as the authors reason or worse, to call this act a *crime* in the modern sense of the term, is quite far-fetched and is, as I pointed out before, just another 'intropretation' of an ancient tale that betrays the bias of the interpreter.

I have to resign here from further interpretation as I got long ago a strong feeling that this myth was construed as a teaching tale, and as such would not to be qualified as a myth that grew organically within a culture, to reflect the mores of that culture. This story is either misconstrued or it was reconstrued later on to fit the morals of our modern epoch.

What I intuitively feel about this strange tale of human madness is that it teaches that patriarchy as a social paradigm doesn't work and creates havoc in all possible relationships, parent-child, husband-spouse, and ruler-citizen. I feel that the actors on the stage are not playing their own selves, but *social roles*. The roles they are playing are cultural clichés.

The question I was asking to myself when I once read this tale for the first time was: 'How would I react if I received such an oracle?' And I found I would ask myself: 'What have I done that I receive such a bad and fatal oracle?'

With this quest for self-knowledge, I would try to find out who I am, what my roots are, what my parents have thought when they conceived me, and what the circumstances were of my birth.

Had Oedipus asked these questions, he would with high probability have returned to Corinth to seriously find out the truth about his origins by questioning his adoptive parents. And if he had been honest, serious and committed, there is again a chance they would have told him the true story. And with this opening of his consciousness, the spell of the oracle would have lost a lot, if not all of its power.

The very act of inquiry, the quest for *self-knowledge*, is exactly what appeases the anger of even the most revengeful gods, and this is why above the gate of the Apollo temple in Delphi, visible for everyone who visits the oracle, is written:

—*Know Thyself!*

But ancient patriarchy as today's consumer culture, which is but a modernized vintage of it, are against the inner quest, and do not teach children what self-inquiry means and how it can be carried out. And this is, after all, the greatest pitfall of this *cultural perversion* we use to call patriarchy.

And to come back to Freud, I must note that I am not ahead in my inquiry why he chose this tale for exemplifying the child's psychosexual growth. I can only guess that Freud chose this tale for exemplifying the modern child's neurosis, or potential neurosis, the modern child's cultural and individual neurosis that namely results from a *deeply schizophrenic* cultural setup.

Dr. Françoise Dolto (1908-1988), the late Freudian psychoanalyst who one of the worlds most reputed child therapists, capable of healing psychotic children, said in one of her workshops on child psychoanalysis that most young psychoanalysts forget about the fact that only the neurotic child is incestuously fixated upon their parents, or the parent of the opposite sex, but not the normal and psychically healthy child.

—See Françoise Dolto, Séminaire de psychanalyse d'enfants, Tome 2 (1985).

If I could, I would ask her: 'What about the percentage of children born in modern consumer culture that are really psychically healthy in the sense that they are fully sexual without being psychosexually attracted to their parents?' My own guess is, perhaps ten percent.

So I am back at where I started, knowing what I knew before, that is, that a culture is mad that arranges family in a way that incestuous fixations are going to be a rampant problem. That they are rampant in our culture was indeed Dolto's view, and her view was based upon almost lifelong professional experience. In her book *La Cause des Enfants (1985)*, she writes:

> In the nuclear family of today, especially in urban areas, the tensions and conflicts are much more explosive, and this is so because they are underlying. Today, the number of persons a child is in touch with is more restrained than formerly. In the 17th and 18th centuries, the child could transfer their incestuous feelings toward other women than their mothers who enjoyed to play little funny sex games with little boys or young people of whom they were not the mother. (Id., 29, Translation mine)

So what am I to do? Blame psychoanalysis? That sounds like blaming the messenger for the message he brings. Freud analyzed his culture. He did not create a new culture. He did not want to change what he saw was an insane culture that brings more evil than good with its moralism, its wars and taboos. He said his mission as a psychiatrist was to heal those who suffer from the pathologies this culture quite inevitably brings about, not more, and not less. But I do not need to follow Freud here, but can become an activist for a new society where children enjoy sexual freedom.

Of course, I can take the position that Wilhelm Reich at the time took against Freud, who admitted and recognized his cultural imbeddedness. Reich argued that we are not the victims of the culture that brought us about, but that we bound to help changing a culture we see is based on principles that stir madness and chaotic behavior in humans.

I personally agree with Reich, while Freud was not wrong after all. He only was conservative. That was his choice.

I am ahead one step, a tiny step though. I know that I can heal people who suffer from the pathologies this culture creates, and I know also that I can help changing this culture. And more importantly, I know that for doing the latter, I cannot harness the power of psychoanalysis. As a matter of common sense, for changing my culture, I must go beyond analyzing it, or proving it wrong. I must show a better way, and I do this first of all by changing myself. What does that imply?

I already mentioned one part of it: find out who I am, what my origins are, what my individual and family karma is. And also, what my talents are, my unique gifts, what my creative potential is like, if it's mathematical, visual, literary, or artistic, if it's good for a career in design, in painting, the performing arts, in science, or in philology, or if I am manually gifted, to become an artisan, or a pianist.

The next part would be to see what my *spiritual orientation* is, what I personally understand under *spirituality* and what I can take from the waters religions offer, or what I cannot take from them. I may choose to craft to my own religion, my own liberal or not so liberal spirituality.

And what happens when I do that? I not only gain self-knowledge, I also help changing my culture.

Explain it as a morphogenetic response or in any other way, fact is that all we individually achieve is an achievement also for the whole of our culture. Thus we impact upon culture, and, incrementally help that culture to reform itself, to change, to transform into a better, more conscious and more harmonious culture in the future.

For example, when I have suffered early child trauma, I will seek out advice and try to cope with what I see are consequences of my fixation, and I may become aware of the fact that this deep early hurt created anxiety and a constriction of my emonic flow.

So I need to get to terms with my body and my bioenergetic setup, by trying to have a harmonious sex life that is as much as possible free of hurt inflicted to others, as much as possible free of anxiety, and as much as possible free of compulsion.

So I will not obey to what society tells me because I know it's wrong and abject because it's society's setup itself that has brought about abuse in the first place; hence, I will opt for free and consenting erotic relationships that I feel are okay for me and my partners—whatever their age.

This is the way of the true hero. In the next chapters I am going to explore the more convoluted ways of the *Oedipal Hero*. And then you may see for yourself which is the better way for you. You can choose what kind of hero you want to be, a true hero or a false hero. Oedipus was the latter.

The true hero integrates self-knowledge, the fake hero, or *Oedipal Hero*, does without. That's really the only difference.

But that tiny difference in our inner setup, in our basic worldview, our attitude, our orientation, you are going to see in the following pages, makes a huge difference in the world, in what the person brings about, as fruits, as karma.

To condense it, I'd say that the true hero creates human progress and evolution while the *Oedipal Hero* creates denial, stuckness, stifled evolution or devolution.

Why this is so is quite easy to understand. The true hero's mission, as it is based upon *conscious choices* brings about an increase of humanity's consciousness.

The *Oedipal Hero's* mission, as it is based upon *unconscious choices* is to decrease, and veil further, humanity's consciousness. In still easier terms, the true hero brings more light to the shadows, while the *Oedipal Hero* brings more shadow to the light. You could also say that the *Oedipal Hero* is the counterplayer to human evolution, and was historically always prominent in times of fascism, political restoration, religious tyranny and the retrogradation of true spirituality into fundamentalist religious fanaticism.

THE OEDIPAL HERO

The Perpetrator Elucidated

It may still not be clear what an *Oedipal Hero* actually is, so I need to further elucidate what characterizes a man or woman who actually is an *Oedipal Hero*.

As a matter of terminology, the woman-type, according to the Freudian expression, should be called *Electra Hero*, but I may simplify matters, or rather restrict the topic of this book to the male vintage of our Oedipus. I think it's wiser to leave it over to a woman to write the other half of the story! I namely argue with the I Ching that self-restraint is a virtue rather than a vice as far as knowledge is concerned.

To be true, I am not possessing the emotional knowledge to write the other part, as I do not *feel* what it is to be a woman, and any man who does is a liar. And this is especially true regarding our hot melting sexual feelings; a man can only speculate how a little girl experiences love for her father, and here is where science finds its natural limitation. Science is not objective and will never be, and a man who explores a woman's sexual universe will never be a real scientist! Period.

This is why, at this point of the study, I am going to deliberately restrict the scope of the study, and explore further on about the *male* vintage of the *Oedipal Hero* only. And hereby, I imply that there is of course a female version of the tale, and I do invite female authors to venture into writing the other half of the moon.

Yet I dare to utter that there is a difference still. The mother-son relation can hardly be compared with the father-daughter relation because the male is more fragile on a psychic level, and therefore mother-son codependence is more devastating for healthy psychosexual growth of a boy than is father-daughter codependence for the psychosexual growth of a girl. This is recognized by most psychologists, psychoanalysts and psychiatrists today; this insight also is part of perennial philosophy and it is *not a sexist view.* The male and female sexes are not construed in the same way on the psychic level, a fact that has been demonstrated time and again in times of crisis, war and social upheaval. Women simply are stronger and more psychically robust than men. They live longer, are less prone to heart disease, chronic fatigue and depression disorders, and can cope better with stress, both in the work place and at home. Of course, as always, exceptions confirm the rule.

But I am thinking of women who love not small boys but little girls erotically, and I am wondering what the etiology of their sexual orientation is. Some of these women have talked about their feelings on the Internet, but they have not speculated about what made them little girls as love mates over little boys. I speculate that it has to do with the specific manner they have lived their *Electra Complex,* how they related or did not relate, or *could* not relate, to their fathers. All is still open in this intriguing research field; little is known because these women are very secretive. I have written emails to some of them, but they did not reply, and I heard of friends they disclosed their feelings to no males, but only to females; which is sexism on the other half of the moon, but okay. I think to advance theoretical reasoning and intellectual deductions on what characterizes the *Oedipal Hero* would be a tedious endeavor. Instead, let me discuss the problem by using teaching tales or examples.

As I do not wish to importunate anybody, I will construe examples from the living material, and leave it over to the reader to see parallels to any known person of the past or of present times.

To begin with, the main characteristic of the *Oedipal Hero* is his lack of self-knowledge. He ignores his true identity. He does not know anything or very little about his roots, and has build a worldview that is not unlike a torso. He has left out from his basic life philosophy all that would betray his true identity, so he rejects karmic astrology, any kind of divination, and also any kind of lesser esoteric knowledge that could inform him about himself. In one word, he rejects truth, true knowledge, and construes a science that delivers him the half-truths that comfort him in his pitiful spiritual ignorance.

In the same way as Oedipus did not reason after receiving the oracle in order to find the truth of that strange prediction within himself, and thus within his destiny, he goes out to save the world from evil, and here is where his pseudo-heroic quest starts.

In the same way as Oedipus did not even think of journeying to Corinth to investigate his origins, the *Oedipal Hero* murders his father, metaphorically speaking, by denying his origins and his karma.

He betrays himself, and his biological, spiritual and genetic roots by reasoning that he 'never had a father,' that he was growing up 'in a females-only household,' that he had 'nothing in common' with his father, as his father was 'a lost soul,' 'a drinker' or a 'social freak,' 'clochard' or 'inept,' a 'secret homosexual' or 'hidden pedophile,' an 'eternal student,' 'hopeless philosopher' or 'eternal abuser' or simply, 'somebody who should never have married and put a child in the world.'

All these variations of the theme 'father' surge up in dialogues with *Oedipal Heroes*, which are in real life to be found in dialogues with those who either got a problem with society, with rules, with authority, or who are on a spiritual-only track.

The latter group of males is interesting because in rejecting their father, they more precisely reject life, the juice of it, pleasure, sensuality, and emotional intelligence, replacing it by a rigid and dogmatic system of fundamentalist beliefs. Thus we got the social-inept, the home-sitters and misanthropes, the revolted ones who want to blow up the system, if they call themselves terrorists or not, and we got the dictators and tyrants who want to punish the world as a projective act for punishing their inadequate fathers.

And we got the child killers who want to punish little girls or boys for not being 'nice enough' to them when they play out their unresolved father imago with the implicit but unvoiced question 'Am I not lovable?' and we got, last not least, the social activist for any 'good cause' for teaching the world what 'real goodness' is all about.

All of them are *Oedipal Heroes*, only that society in its eternal stupidity finds the latter vintage okay and all the other vintages not okay. Society, while not reflecting about the difference, worships the positive

Oedipal Hero while it despises its negative counterpart.

Society somehow understands that both characters have in common that they had a hard childhood, but mainstream society sees a sign of strength and virtue in the fact that a person denies his wound instead of understanding that real strength is to *acknowledge* one's wound.

Society does generally not see that both the positive and the negative *Oedipal Hero* are hurting others, only that the criminal, the schizophrenic and the terrorist do it openly and as it were honestly, and the fake hero, the social activist who becomes a persecutor, fundamentalist, spy, world puritan and ruthless policeman does it covertly and in a projective manner. He hurts those he slaughters in the name of 'doing good.'

The sane mind does not need to save anybody. He does not need to go out for wars against prostitution, child abuse, women's rights or whatever hits his mind. He accepts the world because he accepts himself. And he accepts himself because *he has accepted his origins, his father, and his karma.*

The main characteristic, thus, of the *Oedipal Hero*, compared to the true hero is that he does not know who he is and why he does what he does. He believes he is doing good for others and the world, following a rather mechanistic scheme of values and good-and-bad judgments he has internalized when he was the good boy for his mom. As a result, his behavior code is rather rigid, and his mindset is judgmental. He sees the world divided in the good guys and the bad guys, like in a movie, and his political opinions are following this black-and-white scheme of extreme judgmentalism.

The psychological reason for the *Oedipal Hero* being often simplistic, harsh, clear-cut, dry and judgmental in his evaluation of the world, and human action, is that he needs to defend the insight that life's complexity is smarter than him, telling him, one way or the other, the fake-reasons he is acting for, and what his true motivations are. He intuits that this, in turn, would get him quite automatically on the track of self-inquiry, and that he would by and by find out about his origins, and his karma.

The truth is that life always guides us to gain more self-knowledge and a person must really be rigid beyond reason and judgmental and projective in their overall attitude that this *natural quest for self-knowledge* is completely cut-off. It means the person needs to invest vital energy to uphold the denial structure and the array of projects it has created.

And here we are at the core of the etiology of neurosis as Freud and others have described it. It's a denial of desire, the *desire for knowledge* that is inherent in all living, and it's this denial of knowledge that is the true reason why the person denies sexual engagements, because *sex with others brings knowledge.* While masturbation or autoerotic sex doesn't. Only intercourse brings this knowledge; it is highly significant that the word is also used for denoting social intercourse. It brings knowledge both about our mate and ourselves. This truth is beautifully expressed in the Bible where sexual intercourse is described as 'carnal knowledge' or when it is said that a man is going to *know* a women when he goes in to his wife or concubine. It has often been said that the Hebrew's prohibition of masturbation had procreational reasons, but it may also have been an encouragement to seek intercourse in the sense of 'going out and multiply' as a matter of social communication, instead of staying home and masturbating one's soul off in dreadful solitude.

The number one reason why free sexuality was historically forbidden to slaves is that it brings knowledge. In ancient Greece, for example, *boylove*, the erotic and passionate love of adolescent boys, was permitted only to noble men, not to slaves. A slave who would arrogate to engage in a love relation with a boy would have been jailed.

Another well-known example is the Christian Church. The taboo on sexuality outside the marriage bed and procreation was a powerful aid in the Church's quest for spiritual dominion and control; the Church enforced this taboo draconically, by using threat, persecution, torture and deliberate murder, during the *Inquisition*. The result was a populace that was highly ignorant, and is in wide parts still today, for example about *natural contraception*, while before the holocaust committed by the Inquisition, this knowledge was freely available from midwives and witch doctors.

—See, for example, Riane Eisler, Sacred Pleasure (1996), with further references.

By the same token, the rationale behind the child being today prohibited to engage in sexual relations with peers and adults outside of the family *is to keep children ignorant as long as possible* in order to safeguard consumer culture's dominion and to insure that, as they are starved emotionally and sexually, they become avid and brainless consumers. The present stronghold of multinational business over people's bodies and minds would be impossible to maintain if children grew up knowledgeable about natural copulation from early in life.

And here we may further understand that the *Oedipal Hero* really is a *masturbator* in every sense of the word, sexually, and also metaphorically in the sense of rubbing himself against himself, thereby avoiding the warm company of others.

This latter characteristic forms part of his self-enclosing narcissism, and is not evidently related to his Oedipal fixation. The *Oedipal Hero* is a brilliant masturbator also in front of others, when it goes to hold speeches where he can ejaculate all his poison against his particular scapegoat target.

The other main characteristic of the *Oedipal Hero* is that, much to his own ignorance, he is a *repressed pedophile*. He has strongly repressed and condemned his pedophile urges, to a point to forget his initial attraction somewhere around adolescence and early adulthood. Instead of asking what makes him desire children, and because of fear and guilt, he prefers to shut the door to that inner world and rejects the whole of that itching need for closeness with children; this is how, as a matter of *bioenergetic retrogradation,* he becomes a pedophile-hater and persecutor.

The pedophile differs from the *Oedipal Hero* in that he is conscious of his desire for emotional and sexual closeness with children, and he more or less accepts it. But there are also pedophiles who have not really accepted the choice they have made unconsciously, cursing their fate to be among a sexual minority that is the most despised of all; these half-cooked pedophiles are often also half-cooked *Oedipal Heroes.* I have known a number of exemplars of this vintage and saw them invariably engaged in humanitarian activities for destitute, poor or orphan children, but they strongly condemn in themselves and others every hint of erotic attraction for a child, and when they see other pedophiles acting out, they strike, and denounce them!

All *Oedipal Heroes*, fully or half baked, have in common that they are out to prove the world how strong, good, righteous, courageous, tough and determined they are, and they tend to emphasize that they do not do what they do for selfish reasons, but for 'making a difference,' for helping 'change the world,' or making 'a significant contribution.' It is the rhetoric of selfishness being bad, and altruism being good, of *egoism versus altruism*, of *ego versus beyond*, and all the simplistic spiritual gimmick we know from fundamentalist religions.

They have as it were customized that rhetoric for justifying their persecutor if not terminator spirit that lets them be eternally on guard, like the proverbial baboon, with an erect phallus, to spy out the bad guys and punish them by painful anal rape—at least in their fantasies. (Most of them will do male rape within the range of legalized persecution, thus in most cases by calling law enforcement, but some of them do rape physically, when they happen to be in jail and can spy out sex offenders). As a matter of fantasy, and because they repress a good part of their genitality, they are often regressed into anality, which makes them not very cosy to have around, as they are never relaxed, always constipated, dutifully busy, always on guard, always ready to strike, always charged with emotions they have never learnt to handle.

In their relations with women, these males are most often rough, as they are confused about what tenderness means, and believe a 'real man' had to be smelly, rough and always 'on top,' also sexually. At home, they hardly ever take care of the children as they believe indoor activities are for females, and that males have to win the bread—most of the time.

They most of all abhor imposing females, and a female is dominating already for them when she doesn't want to follow but got her own opinions. Then, she is found 'opinionated.' When she refuses to be beaten for daily little critter, she is found 'emancipated.' When she likes beauty and an aesthetic home, she is called 'extravagant.' When she is tender, sweet and caring with the children, she is called 'a hen.' Beware she is a beautiful woman; she will be constantly supposed to have an affair! And when she did have an affair and is found out, she is called 'a loose cunt' and cast out.

Oedipal Heroes are often to be found in rough sports such as boxing or car racing, and they definitely are the species that populates our gymnasia, and that need to order extra size for the suit, simply as a matter of muscular hypertrophy. They obviously prefer bodybuilding over mind-building, and they are increasingly to be found in politics, where mind was notoriously never asked for. Intellectually *Oedipal Heroes* tend to be mediocre, while they may invest a good time in learning and study, even when adult. When around brilliant people, people at home in academia, or geniuses, they tend to feel inadequate, inferior, ridden with a complex to be intellectual inferior, not smart enough, or to lack conversational abilities, which results in their poor attitude when around on parties, receptions or gala diners.

Regarding manners, they are rather unpolished and tend to come and go in company, so as to have some backup in case they commit a *faux pas*. They abhor to dress well and then go alone to a reception, or they simply avoid it. They are the stuff of dreams of naive country girls, and they have made their fame on the back of that kind of populace, especially in Hollywood drama. Their clumsiness when being around in good society is taken for the charm of the eternal youth, the adolescent charming guy, the *Peter Pan* of the fairies, the *puer* archetype.

They have helped decisively in forming the *American Dream*, and in the glamorous world of Hollywood movies they are stage requisites. The hidden side of the *Oedipal Hero's* glory, his glorious goodness, is his abysmal violence. In most cases, *Oedipal Heroes* are aware of their problem with controlling their anger, their violent outbursts and temper tantrums, and their overall rather revengeful behavior. As if they waited for an opportunity to get mad and run amok, so as to prove themselves that they are *real men.*

The other side of the moon is well to be seen in the movie Dr. Jeckill and Mr. Hyde that shows the schizophrenic nature of the *Oedipal Hero* in a beautifully staged and orchestrated manner. Here the good doc, there the bad dick, two sides of the same medal, as the good citizen transforms into the bad animal-man in a matter of seconds.

Nature is indeed revengeful to those who repress their true nature, and they are controlled by the *inner selves* they disown. In repressing our *pedoemotions* or, generally speaking, in replacing love by moralism, which is the bad choice the *Oedipal Hero* did and where he acted against his better nature, his better knowledge and his higher consciousness, he became deeply fragmented, to a point, in some pathological cases, that the personality splits apart and two separate split personalities emerge.

But what the film shows, and what good psychiatry can equally demonstrate, the split is already there in the Oedipally fixated character, and as a matter of cultural choice, this split is also part of our culture.

Which is why I call it an *Oedipal Culture.*

While we see *Oedipal Heroes* acting out on the public stage virtually every day, as they are so popular, and increasingly popular, we see only their light, and not their shadow. We see only what they do and say officially, not what they do and say in private, and behind closed doors.

We are not supposed to know about it because we would be shocked!

Narcissus and Oedipus

A Complex Psychiatric Problem

This brings me to explain the narcissistic hangup of the *Oedipal Hero*, his extreme narcissism. The authors of *The Mythic Journey* talk about the 'tragedy of narcissistic love.' In understanding the *Oedipal Hero's* narcissism, we will understand his destructiveness, and more specifically, we will begin to see why he is out to destroy love wherever he meets with it. Liz Greene and Juliet Sharman-Burke write:

> This sad myth from Greece tells of passion and rejection, and shows how retaliation and revenge, far from bringing relief, only increase the agony. More importantly, it implies that if we do not know ourselves, we may spend our lives seeking this knowledge through self-obsession—which means that we are not able to offer love to others. (Id., 124)

Narcissism really is not what most lay people understand under this header. It is not self-love, but the very contrary of it. Narcissus was deaf to the whispers of the nymph Echo not because he loved himself too much, but because he was self-obsessed. Self-obsession is not self-love, it is a compensation of their inner vacuum, which is a lack of self-knowledge, and also a total lack of true spirituality. *It is a loss of soul.* We cannot love another when our lives are soulless, and meaningless, when we lack spiritual orientation in life, when we don't know who we really are.

Narcissists, and also those who have the double affliction of an Oedipal hangup together with a narcissistic fixation, that is, *Oedipal Heroes,* are understanding many things under the header of love. They understand that it may allow one to control another, to take advantage of another, to be comforted in lonely moments, to have a wife that bears children, or children who care for one in old age—which are all utilitarian concepts of love. He may foster other concepts of love, but they are all not love, but conceptual molds for something they do not understand. They are fingers that point to the moon, but not the moon, as the Zen saying goes. And what most narcissists most want when they say they love somebody is fulfillment, satisfaction, emotional and sexual, and often also material satisfaction. 'I have one wife and two children. I have a family. I have a home. I have company. I have security. I have comfort. I have.' The *Oedipal Hero* is fully on the side of what Erich Fromm called *To Have* and very little or not at all on the side of *To Be*. He believes a life of true *To Be* is reserved to artists, children and life coaches. For him, love must have a *reason*. And if it has none, he will give one to it. The *Oedipal Hero* virtually bathes in conceptual thinking; the idea that life may be something to be truly perceived only when doing away with all concepts and put up a direct connection is an alien idea to him.

I have got the proof of these facts many times in my life, in relations with *Oedipal Heroes*, most of the time those who worship a social ideal, and who are violently against alcohol and consciousness-altering compounds. These people regularly suffer from depressions, experience constant drawbacks in relationships, and most of them complain about hard-to-control sexual urges. When I suggest to them to once go and look over the fence of their senseless activism by going on a discovery journey, either by using *Ayahuasca* or by doing some real spiritual work on their etheric bodies, I get the answer that they are invariably 'against esoterism,' 'against new ageism,' 'against drugs' and 'against daydreamerism.'

The ending -ism most often appears in their diction. One wrote about my Encyclopedia, he found it quite good but could not understand my 'mysticism and spiritualism,' as he expressed himself. When I pointed him to his need for love in his relationships, and affirmed that love given was most often returned, he said he had no sense for 'so much lovism.' And in subsequent mails he would come up with reasons why love does not exist and can never exist with the human race, that love was but a 'religious idea' or an intellectual concept, and nothing real.

The most offensive of *Oedipal Heroes*, in my view, are the spies. I have discovered a number of them in the rings of the pedophile movement, and what is typical about them is that they want to appear *more pedophile than pedophile* to attract the attention of those who are *really* pedophile. They themselves, be they outright police spies, be they half-baked pedophiles who are not clear about their feelings and how they can cope with them, constantly are to be found in search of contact with pedophiles, usually via online forums and mailing lists, where they implore their 'affliction' and ask others how to cope with it, or if suicide was perhaps the best solution?

What they are really searching for is love and understanding. They want to be loved and chose to mix with one of the most persecuted minorities so as to get attention and consolation of their inner emptiness, and their more or less total spiritual ignorance. They may have felt an attraction once to a little boy or girl, adolescent or child, and derive from such a single event a conclusion of 'being a pedophile' while they otherwise completely ignore what this means and implies. Which is just another typical habit they often engage in: jumping to conclusions with a tidbit of knowledge, or in total ignorance of what they are actually talking about.

The reason is *boomeritis*. They pick up whatever they find fashionable and *cool*, be it something others frown upon, if only they can make a difference by indulging in it and pretending to be this-and-that. So doing will for a certain while fill their inner emptiness; they have something to gossip and rant about.

As to the facts, I have largely expanded about what is, and what is not pedophile attraction in other publications; the fact of having a one-time or transitory sexual attraction for a child by no means implies the person to being pedophile and still less to being 'a pedophile.'

> —It has to be noted that there is no one-type singular clear-cut definition of the personality of 'The Pedophile;' there are only pedophiles, and each has a different psychic setup, as every heterosexual or homosexual. It is one of the most sordid polemic bursts of the mass media to suggest there was something like a one-dimensional definition of 'The Pedophile' as a distinct character type. This kind of polemics leads straight to euthanasia, and that is why it should be prohibited by law in a democracy.

I have particularly elucidated that we all have *pedoemotions*, which means loving feelings for children that may or not become sexualized.

While *pedoemotions* are universal, pedophiles are special in that their sexual attraction has crystallized into something exclusive; their emosexual focus is on children, and here even more particularly upon a specific age group and gender of children, not just children as a generic group. Pedophile attraction is not random, but *specific*.

A favorite modern-day subject *Oedipal Heroes* rant about is pedophilia, or rather what they project upon it. And it's no better when it's about their own supposed pedophilia, when in truth they are hooked up in a shallow normalcy and are looking for a girlfriend, a young women, but dare not approach one, coward as they are. Interestingly so, Sigmund Freud must have known some exemplars of this vintage, but he was gross and unscientific when *generalizing* that male pedophilia generally was but cowardice to approach an adult female. In that general sense, Freud's statement is blunder, but with regard to this specific group of *Oedipal Heroes* I mentioned, it is true.

Oedipal Heroes bear their narcissistic wound often in public, like one bears an amulet; this is especially today the practice in the United States and in the American media world; narcissism, as it's the fashionable affliction of a whole nation, has become a sign of class. Thomas Moore says in his bestselling book *Care of the Soul* that America has a great longing to be the *New World* of opportunity and a moral beacon for the world.

—Thomas Moore, Care of the Soul (1994), 62.

And further:

It longs to fulfill these narcissistic images of itself. At the same time it is painful to realize the distance between the reality and that image. America's narcissism is strong. It is paraded before the world. If we were to put the nation on the couch, we might discover that narcissism is its most obvious symptom. And yet that narcissism holds the promise that this all-important myth can find its way into life. In other words, America's narcissism is its refined puer spirit of genuine new vision. The trick is to find a way to that water of transformation where hard self-absorption turns into loving dialogue with the world. (Id.)

In a way, narcissists suffer not only from their own emotional starvation, and their inner lack of love, but also, and more importantly, from the love and the emotions they try to attack, invalidate and make down in others. This terrible *reductionism* breeds destructiveness that they pay for by being increasingly nihilistic and depressive, the older they get. Accordingly, Thomas Moore observes:

Narcissism has no soul. In narcissism we take away the soul's substance, its weight and importance, and reduce it to an echo of our own thoughts. There is no such thing as the soul. We say. It is only the brain going through electrical and chemical changes. Or it is only behavior. Or it is only memory and conditioning. (Id., 58-59)

The authors of *The Mythic Journey* comment that 'The unhappy love lives of many public icons testimony to this voracious hunger for love which is meant to replace what was missing early in life – a sense of being real as oneself.' In a society that has since long lost every notion of what love truly is, because it has killed love, it is no wonder that it has become a fashion to *speculate love was just a concept,* and there was nothing behind but rhetoric, and that what religions suppose is love is not.

Many males in our sensually deprived postmodern neo-patriarchy believe love to be a mere concept, a word, a religious idea, or a rose-colored birthday card, because they really never experienced how love feels! As children they were not loved, not desired, because they had busy parents, parents who were interested in money-making, science or banking, but not in the children they procreated. Thus, here is their huge narcissistic wound, as they grew into a life that was basically felt as cold and hostile, as they have felt their parents to be eternally absentminded, when they really needed their warmth, their closeness, their touch, their kisses, their strokes and fondling, their love expressed by the body – and not by nice-sounding verbiage. Many of them had probably as parents those *gossiping monsters* that American commercials lavishly portray as the nation's model parents.

In fact, this vintage obviously coins the mold for the mass of shallow-minded individuals who are hostile to touch as they suffer from the culture's bias that assumes that 'all touch is somehow sexual'. They thus embody the politically correct American parent who keeps his hands safely in his pockets! *Noli me tangere!*

I think it would be a miracle when in such a culture a family is *not* habitually violent, *not* schizophrenic, *not* touch-hostile, and where a single child can grow into a healthy and joyful autonomy and self-reliance. *I want to see that child!* You can search for it as the proverbial needle in the hay. For of course the collective picture of a society assembled of a majority of *Oedipal Heroes*, mixed of the male and female vintage, is not your usual healthy collective, but a madhouse.

Postmodern Mix

The Origins of Sexual Violence

In this last chapter, I shall elucidate how the Oedipus and Narcissus sagas hang together, and how this has given the intrinsic taste to today's postmodern consumer culture, which I call synonymously *Oedipal culture, hero culture, paranoid culture, paraculture, incest culture, rape culture, murder culture* or *abuse-centered culture*. I shall focus in this analysis on how the violent impulse comes up to abduct, sexually penetrate and murder young children, and how it is related to both the Oedipal and narcissistic fixations playing in synch, which, then, gives the special postmodern mix of violent moralism.

This problem has never been understood by psychiatry. In the case of the German child killer Jürgen Bartsch, even today German psychiatric authorities exhibit the nonsensical theory of Bartsch having been at the same time 'a pedophile, a pederast and a homosexual.' Which is about as saying that a cauliflower is composed of a tree, an apple and a pear.

As long as Western psychology, psychiatry and sexology do not recognize the *primacy of the emotional etiology in sexual paraphilias* before jumping to look for the culprit in the sexual setup of the person, nothing will be understood here, not even in the future.

I have drafted an approach to healing sexual sadism that focuses on a bioenergetic view and that acknowledges that in every sexual attraction the prime motivating force is *emotional*, and not sexual in the first place. It is this emotional predilection that in some cases becomes sexualized, or charged with sexual energy. The healing of the sadistic affliction, then, is brought about through reactivating the natural *emotional flow* in the organism. Thus, when I want to understand sadism and violent sex crime that is an outflow of this sadism, I must focus on the emotional setup of the person, and inquire if emotions are flowing, or if the emotional flow is blocked.

In fact, sadism can only be understood when the fact is seen that emotions, as a condensation of *élan vital* or *life force*, naturally flow in the healthy organism, and are changing in a kaleidoscopic way, and that every blockage of this flow brings about a violent outburst because the energy will free its way to full discharge. (If the latter is also prohibited by the person's superego, the person will not be a sadist but grow a cancer or throw a heart disease).

I shall develop further along the lines of the Narcissus legend and ask a few questions. According to the myth, Narcissus fell in love with his own self-image. Was he never loved by anyone, or why did he feel such an urge to fall in love, an urge so strong that in absence of any tangible other love object, he chose himself? Since his childhood, his beauty had been admired by everyone.

Narcissus himself, however, who has never seen himself in the mirror, was unaware of his identity. One day, when he walked at the border of a lake which was a virgin lake as no animal had ever drunk from it, and no tree ever plunged its branches in it, and no human had ever seen it. Here, the youngster felt a sudden fatigue. He sat down at the lake and bowed over the water for drinking. And, for the first time, he saw his double. Fallen in love with himself, the myth says, he spent hours in melancholy and in regretting that he would never be able to possess his twin sister, which was his living self-image. Eventually, concludes the tale, Narcissus could not stand the agony of this impossible love and ran a knife in his heart, bursting out in: 'Farewell, beautiful love that has no hope.' And on the place where his blood fell on the ground, white narcissi grew that had red hearts.

This for the legend.

On first sight one may think that this is a story about vanity. But in reality the legend stands for the discovery of *identity*. What is identity? Identity can be defined operationally, as it's very difficult to give an overall definition to it, about as difficult as it is to define love. Functionally speaking, identity is characterized by the fact that all what we can discover in another, we must have discovered in ourselves first.

And the end result of this self-discovery is identity. This means that we cannot perceive the qualities of another if, and as long as, we ignore our own. Narcissus' apparent egocentrism is truly the first step, and a necessary one, in his self-discovery, which is catalyzed by the discovery why he is lovable. Self-love is the condition for our capacity to love others.

This psychological insight must be put in relation to education and the child's relationship with the mother. It is not haphazard that in the legend, the mother took all kinds of precautions to avoid the child discovering himself in a mirror! Such as Narcissus' mother are mothers who have never time and attention for their child. *The mother is the mirror of the child's ego.* The ego can develop only in a child whose mother is able and willing to mirror that ego. A narcissistic mother cannot do that. This is why children who have narcissistic mothers, also called *witch mothers*, do not know who they are, and their ego development is deficient. Such kind of mothers search in their children what they, when they were young, searched in their parents: they try to *mirror themselves in their children*, thereby changing the roles, and the rules, in that they burden the child with an ability a child cannot have, namely to be a parent for their own mother. This results in the child as a later adult having in turn a deficient ego. As it is already obvious after this short explanation, narcissism is by definition generational, really a family curse, to use the old term, and here it's correct, but not for the Oedipal hangup.

The problem of narcissism is especially virulent with single mothers who got a single male child, and when the father of the child is absent forever or most of the time. Here then, in this constellation, as I have shortly outlined earlier in this study, the Oedipal hangup comes in and makes itself felt.

When the boy cannot identify with his father during the Oedipal phase, the boy will develop an Oedipal hangup. That means the boy will cling to his mother in an unhealthy and neurotic manner that will negatively infringe upon his emotional and psychosexual development.

In the legend, Oedipus killed his father and married his mother. He however did this unconsciously, for he ignored his parents. The tragedy was triggered by the father, not the son. If we say it was fate, and only fate, we in last resort deny responsibility. An Oedipal fixation becomes a problem for a little boy especially in case the mother is a home-sitter, a woman who has abandoned any hope to find a viable partner, and thus projects her erotic wishes on her son. This may be expressed in erotically seductive behavior, but in most cases these women are actually erotically blocked on a conscious level. The problem here is that the boy won't leave the home in search of a partner and that the constant emotional demands of the mother trap the boy in a pseudo-incestuous and co-dependent partner relation where he becomes the *ersatz* for the partner the mother denies herself to find.

The fact that such a relation remains platonic is insignificant compared to the impossibility for the boy to truly build autonomy. In this constellation, what happens is that the boy's striving for autonomy either faces explicit demands of the mother to stay close to her, or is charged with guilt and a growing rationalization of the situation that will be expressed by the boy in the wish to 'protect' the mother, to save the mother from any harm she suffered previously with men.

Typically in this entanglement situation, the mother tells her son in all length and width the misfortunes she suffered in her love life, thereby invoking in him a *self-defeating judgment about himself*, his own maleness. This negative judgment of the male can be coarsely expressed in the slogan *'all men are swines'*.

In my own case of co-dependence with my mother, all this was aggravated further through the fact that my mother put me in homes where I was cruelly mistreated, without caring too much about the violence inflicted upon me on a daily basis. This resulted in a particularly strong contradiction between the life I was leading during the week, in the home, and the life I was supposed to live with her, during the weekend; it gave her a basis for justifying her over-protectiveness, and the *home sweet home* philosophy she spun around it. I had to be compensated, she reasoned, for the 'bad home' in having a 'nice weekend' with her and she would, as always, be 'very generous' to me, and it was this so-called 'generosity' that she always forwarded as a shield in situations of conflict, when I namely wanted greater autonomy.

I was of course not unconscious of this sordid entanglement, and here I certainly differed from other youngsters in that I was actually so conscious about it that I actively wished to break out of it and repeatedly thought of running away from home. I was often furious against my mother and had a strong sense of the injustice she was doing to me, but I could not express this anger other than by thinking of myself as being a bad boy.

Later on in life, when I was already married, actually not so much later, as I married young, I reproached my mother to have overprotected me in a way to keep me away from life, thereby invalidating my striving for autonomy, and my quest to make love experiences with girls outside home and school. Her answer in that and other very similar situations was one of viciously attacking me as an ungrateful nerd who was 'just like his father and uncles', while she had 'sacrificed herself always' so that I could have a *decent life* because if I had been under the tutelary authority of my father, I would have 'run the streets to find food'. That she regretted the bad experiences I made in the homes but that she had 'always been much more generous than any other parent', for compensating me a little for the hurt suffered in those homes.

When I asked her, at age eighteen, to study in Paris, she replied she was not going to finance my 'interest for luxury' and that if I wanted to study there, I should 'find my money in the street.' I stayed and studied in my home town. Similarly for the subject to study. I preferred to become a musical teacher or recording engineer, but she insisted law was the best for me to study. I gave in while I knew that I had a passion for music, and for children, and would have to force myself onto law. Which I did for the next twenty years.

Typically, emotional abuse does not imply a sexual interaction between parent and child. In the contrary will the mother carefully avoid touching the boy, and it's this *avoidance of touch* much more than anything that rings the alarm bell in the boy's unconscious. Why does my mother never touch me, he reasons? And correctly so. Why do these mothers never touch their sons, I thus ask again, as the answer is in the question? Emotional abuse is so much ingrained in patriarchal culture, and the role of the mother-saving *Oedipal Hero* is so common in our culture that most people never even once reflect about the perversity of such a family constellation!

Easy body touch is not something fostered in this kind of milieu; in the contrary. It is something fostered in healthy families, where parents have a functional love and sex life. It is the conflict between the never-talked-about and repressed, and the prudishness that results from this repression, on one hand, and the open or implicit possessiveness of the symbiotoholic parent, on the other, that triggers in the child an unconscious sexual response for the parent. The for most people uncomfortable truth is that if the incest had been acted out sexually, the *psychic tension at the root of the co-dependence would not pent up* and no Oedipal fixation would result from it.

Men have given open testimonials on television who had consenting intercourse with their mothers, and the astonishing result was that they had the most fulfilling sex life with adult females later on in life; often in these constellations the future wife will have an excellent relationship with the first woman the boy enjoyed sexually, his mother. It is emotional incest, not sexual incest that really creates havoc in a boy's psyche because his biological male identity is gravely impaired through the exclusiveness of his relation with mother; and guilt and shame is the result of it because the boy knows that he should rather look around for a girl of his age or even an older woman, and that it's time to leave his mother and the nest behind.

I see in this ungainly attitude of narcissistic mothers toward their sons the real core of the problem of emotional abuse because it creates a flagrant contradiction. When the boy wants to go out and look for friends or a girlfriend, the mother will tend to keep him away from life, arguing he was still 'too young and unexperienced' to just go on his own, that there are dangers involved in such a quest, or perverse strangers waiting to get him around the corner. But when it goes to care for mother because she is sick, depressed, or had a bad day, then boy is big enough to play the gigolo, and to be around mother, and at her feet for any service she may need, and boy is big enough then to understand when mother talks about her past and her 'bad experiences with men'. This contradiction creates rage in the boy because he sees that the mother just uses him for her purposes and plays power games with him.

From a bioenergetic point of view, it has to be seen that the Oedipal conflict is traumatic for the child because of the *denial of sexual fulfillment* it implies, while it triggers so much longing in the child. It's a real torture for the child, a real trauma, and it has been admitted by psychoanalyst Françoise Dolto that in most cases children lose their pre-Oedipal memory, which only confirms my assumption that the Oedipal construct in Western culture brings *real trauma* to the child as it results in amnesia. In her book *La Cause des Enfants (1985)*, Dolto writes at 29-30 (Translation mine):

FRANÇOISE DOLTO

Memory in adults erases all that belongs to the pre-oedipal period. That is why our society has so much difficulty to accept infantile sexuality. In past centuries there were the nurses who knew it. Parents, however, ignored it.

Freud namely found that amnesia, the loss of memory subsequent to the trauma-triggering situation is in most cases the indicator for trauma having occurred. Hence, Freud concluded, when we find childhood amnesia in a patient, this can be taken as direct evidence for the etiology of trauma to be affirmed for that situation in question. This is in my view the reason for the strong aggressiveness toward the parent of the same sex, in the Oedipal situation. It's a visceral reaction of the biosystem that comes from sensual and sexual deprivation and that is caused by the exclusiveness of the parent-child relation in general, and parental and societal prohibition of children having sex with peers, in particular.

Children *need and want a sex life*, much like adults, while the sexual acts children perform or attempt to perform may be of a lesser complete nature, but this difference does not alter the psychosexual importance of childhood sexuality.

When, as in our culture, children are prohibited from engaging in sexually explicit and healthy peer relations, or relations with adults other than their parents, they will be trapped, if they want or not, in a *gerontophilic* attraction toward their parents.

This cultural setup that is obviously against nature, results in the triangular relationship between parents and one or two children that is so typical for the modern urban family. In this strongly exclusive and triangular relationship, the child is coerced into an ambiguous love-hate relation with their parents; what fuels the child's aggressiveness toward the parent of the same sex is not, as Freud supposed, a situation of rivalry for the single available sex partner, often coined colloquially as 'two men desire one woman' or 'two girls desire one man', but more generally a rage to have been denied the vast realm of potential sex partners of same or different age, *outside of the family!* And the aggressiveness, therefore, of the child is not exclusively directed against the parent of the same sex, but against both parents, while it has to be noted that the child's organism will not allow the child to gain consciousness of this rage because of mere survival reasons. The child's cognitive apparatus will build in a justification factor that leads to the child's reasoning on the lines of :

—Well, I am supposed to love my parents, and be exclusively loved by my parents, as society does not allow me to love other people, and does not allow other people to love me in the same way as my parents love me. Society says it's dangerous for me, as other people may want to abduct and kill me as they cannot love me in the same pure manner as my parents do.

Here is where the whole system of lies and betrayal starts to distort the perception and cognitive grasp of love by the consumer child, in this bias that society puts up, and that it strongly fuels through its abysmally violent anti-pedophilia debate! And what it leads to is that because children cannot for survival reasons express the rage against their parents and society, they will turn this rage against themselves, and become narcissistic and auto-destructive, if not schizophrenic!

Even children who do not develop a pathology will remain with strong guilt feelings, often all their life through, regarding sexuality and all forms of erotic love.

I guess Freud's reasoning here is true insofar as when the parent of the opposite sex is present, the child can project some of the aggressiveness upon him or her. But here, contrary to Freud, I assume that because of survival reasons, this acting-out of aggressiveness toward the parent of the same sex, for example through straight talk, or by hitting the parent, is such perilous an action for a child that this will be done only when he or she can be sure of the support and unconditional love of the parent of the opposite sex. This is a precarious situation for a child in any kind of family, and I believe that generally Freud's reasoning here was quite theoretical. As a general rule, children do keep true to respecting their parents even to a point of self-denial, except a minority of children who incarnate with a very strong ego and character. I have indeed observed that the number of children of the latter vintage is growing over the last decades, but at the same time, the situation of the child in consumer culture has become more and more tough, and alienating, to a point that children are today as much under state control and supervision as nuclear weapons, foreign embassies, top secret material and spies.

This is a potential root for more domestic violence because to enclose children in homes and schools that function pretty much like prisons is not what a caring state will do who loves their child citizens. We are facing a major social and political pathology here, if we can face it at all.

In my experience, most people in Western culture blind these facts simply out of their consciousness interface, and this because of sheer fright of the consequences of any vital action to the contrary.

Freud's cultural bias is notorious and I will not need to write pages about that as it has not only been analyzed in modern biographies and recent psychoanalytic literature, but it was the true reason for the clash between Freud and Reich, Freud and Jung, Freud and Adler, Freud and Rank, Freud and Klein, and Freud and Fromm.

The clashes were of course personally tinted, and in each case, there was a personal drama behind the scenes.

What is significant however, and common to all of these deep relationships is that none of them was solved peacefully; this already is a hint as to the unruly nature of Freud's authoritarianism. And the material speaks for itself, as we have really a large body of evidence.

The clash between Reich and Freud was particularly revealing, and Freud's cultural bias, for one time, was explicit and coined into the dictum 'culture must prevail'. Freud rejected Reich's activism for child sexual rights, despite the fact that it was he himself, who had for the first time in Western social history openly declared that the human child is sexual from birth. Freud reasoned Reich with the argument that the psychiatric profession had to accept the basic setup of society including its denial of the sexual rights of the child, and that the psychiatrist and psychoanalyst had to cure the psychic malformations resulting from the cultural distortion of the natural sexual function, but not more. In other words, they had to restrain from any social activism because otherwise, as Freud thought, society would be thrown into chaos.

The Oedipal situation, as I coin in one term the whole of the emotional, tactile, sensual and sexual deprivation of the child in modern consumer culture, is a *real trauma*. It creates havoc in the child's psyche and one of the undesired results of this pathology is that it leads to a link between sexual desire, aggressive rage and fear, which can lead to sexual deviations later in life. Typical for these deviations is namely that the person can discharge sexually only if acts of sadism are inflicted upon the mate, or conversely, the masochistic suffering of acts of sadism is experienced during the mating game.

When adult males project their unconscious Oedipal mother imago on little girls, they may experience emotional and sexual attraction for them, but they also may at times experience the same rage they felt toward their mothers, but that they repressed. This repressed rage, then, may become sexually charged. This may, or not, depending on the level of consciousness of the person, lead to a violent urge to punish little girls by beating them up and/or by forcing oral, anal or vaginal intercourse on them, or by abducting them for this purpose. It has since long been established by psychiatry that these urges, be they acted out or not, have their origin in an unresolved *Oedipus Complex*.

The person will have greater control of this affliction if he does not fight it but tries to understand his behavior, and his emotional confusion. And here we see again the difference in behavior between the true hero and the *Oedipal Hero*.

The true hero will first of all acknowledge the desire, be it hard to accept, and hard to live with, and cope with, even if the desire is so virulent that it can never be acted out without really hurting and harming the child physically, or emotionally.

This is, to repeat it, not the case with a pure sexual attraction, as in that case a way can be found in most circumstances to abreact sexually without actual penetration, but only in the aggravating case that the desire is charged with violence in such a way that penetration is needed for coming off, and even worse, that the child has to be beaten, made suffer and cry and give signs of expressing the pain, typically by screaming, for the sadist being able to discharge orgasmically. It goes without saying that for any child, whatever their age, and even an adult, the latter experience is not a particularly nice one, while a tender sexual encounter with an adult without penetration may go along with a child, even a completely innocent boy or girl, if only there is no pain, no violence and no threat, and most importantly, no coercion.

The problem is that most *Oedipal Heroes* in one way or the other suffer from sexual sadism, as a simple result of the rage they repressed when they repeatedly wanted to build autonomy and were held back by their possessive and narcissistic mothers. While society has developed in recent years quite a permissive attitude toward *sadomasochism* when it occurs between *consenting adults*, this form of sexuality remains highly problematic when an adult traps a child into his sadistic affliction, and perhaps by expecting the child to be masochistic 'by nature' in order to justify the offense.

Whatever one may think in this respect, it can hardly be denied that our society must show *more responsibility* in working out future social and legal policies for preventing sexual violence against children. The present situation is not satisfying, as it only focuses upon enforcing time and again criminal punishments, which has never been an effective social policy; one may begin to look at how the situation of the *Oedipal Hero* could be cognitively grasped and understood, and how, as a result of these insights, methods could be developed to help the afflicted men to grow beyond their fixation.

In this endeavor, one focus should certainly be to help the individual to accept to be loved, to be touched, to be kissed and fondled, to begin contemplating himself in a mirror while experiencing feelings of power, self-love, admiration and healthy self-pride.

An important element of the therapy would be to dissolve the muscular and characterological armor, and this by suggesting the person to experience sexual intercourse with a young woman in a loving and tender way, while the focus should be on enjoying the hot and melting energy flow as it streams through the body, once the armor has been dissolved.

My research showed that no coercion can help with sexual sadism, but *only tolerance, and again tolerance*, and teaching the person actually to be tolerant with himself. Tolerance means *patience* first of all, as any progress will be incremental, and rather slow in the beginning. With dissolving the character armor, the entire belief system of the *Oedipal Hero* will bit by bit fall in ashes, and when the mind is enlarged, the body will decrease in size, as a matter of inverse proportionality.

I mean that any pattern of obsessive body-building, obesity, heavy drinking or chain-smoking will vanish by itself, once the armor begins to fall apart. On the other hand, I am not in the rings of those who believe that curing the symptoms will do the job, which is why I am firmly opposed to any kind of quick fixes in this respect. Only a holistic, and inside-out approach can do.

Sadism is not easy to heal, and in mainstream psychiatry's view sadistic child sexual offenders, rapists and killers are still today declared incurable!

POSTFACE

Summary

This brings me to close this article with a hopeful outlook; it was not written in the intention to blame a certain group of people, or to blame any behavior they indulge in, even if they compulsively engage in it.

My intent for writing this booklet was to raise awareness in postmodern international culture for a complex of phenomena that are clearly on the rise because of various factors inherent in modern consumer culture, one of them being an unhealthy exclusiveness in the parent-child relation, another being the turndown of the traditional extended family, another still the shortening or total abandonment of breastfeeding, another the rampant tactile, sensual and sexual deprivation of infants and children and decreasing periods of breastfeeding, and still another the rise of the single-parent family because of rampant divorce rates in all major urban areas worldwide.

I hope that this topic will invoke a larger scientific interest in exploring the possibilities of helping persons with an Oedipal, narcissistic and sadistic affliction to deal effectively with their problems, as this will turn out to be the best way of reducing violent sexual crime against children, wherever in the world.

I especially hope that eventually the fatalistic trend in mainstream forensic psychiatry will give way to a deeper regard on the *real possibilities* that exist now in our society and that existed in tribal societies since millennia for healing sexual and nonsexual sadism.

—See Peter Fritz Walter, Emotional Flow: A Holistic Approach to Healing Sadism (Essays on Law, Policy and Psychiatry, Vol. 4), 2017.

All sexual fixations are the result of emotional stuckness, and can be healed through various methods that enliven the emotional flow and help the person to raise their vital energy potential, thereby overcoming the emotional deadlock.

BIBLIOGRAPHY

Contextual Bibliography

Ariès, Philippe

Centuries of Childhood
New York: Vintage Books, 1962

Arntz, William & Chasse, Betsy

What the Bleep Do We Know
20th Century Fox, 2005 (DVD)

Down The Rabbit Hole Quantum Edition
20th Century Fox, 2006 (3 DVD Set)

Covitz, Joel

Emotional Child Abuse
The Family Curse
Boston: Sigo Press, 1986

DeMause, Lloyd

The History of Childhood
New York, 1974

Foundations of Psychohistory
New York: Creative Roots, 1982

Diamond, Stephen A., May, Rollo

Anger, Madness, and the Daimonic
The Psychological Genesis of Violence, Evil and Creativity
New York: State University of New York Press, 1999

DiCarlo, Russell E. (Ed.)

Towards A New World View
Conversations at the Leading Edge
Erie, PA: Epic Publishing, 1996

Dolto, Françoise

La Cause des Enfants
Paris: Laffont, 1985

Psychanalyse et Pédiatrie
Paris: Seuil, 1971

Séminaire de Psychanalyse d'Enfants, 1
Paris: Seuil, 1982

Séminaire de Psychanalyse d'Enfants, 2
PARIS: SEUIL, 1985

Séminaire de Psychanalyse d'Enfants, 3
PARIS: SEUIL, 1988

L'évangile au risque de la psychanalyse
PARIS: SEUIL, 1980

EISLER, RIANE

The Chalice and the Blade
OUR HISTORY, OUR FUTURE
SAN FRANCISCO: HARPER & ROW, 1995

Sacred Pleasure: Sex, Myth and the Politics of the Body
NEW PATHS TO POWER AND LOVE
SAN FRANCISCO: HARPER & ROW, 1996

The Partnership Way
NEW TOOLS FOR LIVING AND LEARNING
WITH DAVID LOYE
BRANDON, VT: HOLISTIC EDUCATION PRESS, 1998

The Real Wealth of Nations
CREATING A CARING ECONOMICS
SAN FRANCISCO: BERRETT-KOEHLER PUBLISHERS, 2008

ELLIS, HAVELOCK

Sexual Inversion
REPUBLISHED
NEW YORK: UNIVERSITY PRESS OF THE PACIFIC, 2001
ORIGINALLY PUBLISHED IN 1897

The Sexual Impulse in Women
REPUBLISHED
NEW YORK: UNIVERSITY PRESS OF THE PACIFIC, 2001
ORIGINALLY PUBLISHED IN 1903

The Dance of Life
NEW YORK: GREENWOOD PRESS REPRINT EDITION, 1973
ORIGINALLY PUBLISHED IN 1923

ELWIN, V.

The Muria and their Ghotul
BOMBAY: OXFORD UNIVERSITY PRESS, 1947

ERICKSON, MILTON H.

My Voice Will Go With You
THE TEACHING TALES OF MILTON H. ERICKSON
BY SIDNEY ROSEN (ED.)
NEW YORK: NORTON & CO., 1991

Complete Works 1.0, CD-ROM
NEW YORK: MILTON H. ERICKSON FOUNDATION, 2001

FREUD, SIGMUND

The Interpretation of Dreams
NEW YORK: AVON, REISSUE EDITION, 1980
AND IN: THE STANDARD EDITION OF THE COMPLETE PSYCHOLOGICAL
WORKS OF SIGMUND FREUD , (24 VOLUMES) ED. BY JAMES STRACHEY
NEW YORK: W. W. NORTON & COMPANY, 1976

Totem and Taboo
NEW YORK: ROUTLEDGE, 1999
ORIGINALLY PUBLISHED IN 1913

FROMM, ERICH

The Anatomy of Human Destructiveness
NEW YORK: OWL BOOK, 1992
ORIGINALLY PUBLISHED IN 1973

Escape from Freedom
NEW YORK: OWL BOOKS, 1994
ORIGINALLY PUBLISHED IN 1941
TO HAVE OR TO BE
NEW YORK: CONTINUUM INTERNATIONAL PUBLISHING, 1996
ORIGINALLY PUBLISHED IN 1976

The Art of Loving
NEW YORK: HARPERPERENNIAL, 2000
ORIGINALLY PUBLISHED IN 1956

GOLEMAN, DANIEL

Emotional Intelligence
NEW YORK, BANTAM BOOKS, 1995

GORDON, ROSEMARY

Pedophilia: Normal and Abnormal
IN: KRAEMER, THE FORBIDDEN LOVE
LONDON, 1976

GOSWAMI, AMIT

The Self-Aware Universe
HOW CONSCIOUSNESS CREATES THE MATERIAL WORLD
NEW YORK: TARCHER/PUTNAM, 1995

GROTH, A. NICHOLAS

Men Who Rape
THE PSYCHOLOGY OF THE OFFENDER
NEW YORK: PERSEUS PUBLISHING, 1980

HAMEROFF, NEWBERG, WOOLF, BIERMAN

Consciousness
20 SCIENTISTS INTERVIEWED
DIRECTOR: GREGORY ALSBURY
5 DVD BOX SET, 540 MIN.
NEW YORK: ALSBURY FILMS, 2003

JAMES, WILLIAM

Writings 1902-1910
THE VARIETIES OF RELIGIOUS EXPERIENCE / PRAGMATISM / A PLURALISTIC
UNIVERSE / THE MEANING OF TRUTH / SOME PROBLEMS OF PHILOSOPHY /
ESSAYS
NEW YORK: LIBRARY OF AMERICA, 1988

JUNG, CARL GUSTAV

Archetypes of the Collective Unconscious
IN: THE BASIC WRITINGS OF C.G. JUNG
NEW YORK: THE MODERN LIBRARY, 1959, 358-407

Collected Works
NEW YORK, 1959

On the Nature of the Psyche
IN: THE BASIC WRITINGS OF C.G. JUNG
NEW YORK: THE MODERN LIBRARY, 1959, 47-133

Psychological Types
COLLECTED WRITINGS, VOL. 6
PRINCETON: PRINCETON UNIVERSITY PRESS, 1971

Psychology and Religion
IN: THE BASIC WRITINGS OF C.G. JUNG
NEW YORK: THE MODERN LIBRARY, 1959, 582-655

Religious and Psychological Problems of Alchemy
IN: THE BASIC WRITINGS OF C.G. JUNG
NEW YORK: THE MODERN LIBRARY, 1959, 537-581

The Basic Writings of C.G. Jung
NEW YORK: THE MODERN LIBRARY, 1959

The Development of Personality
COLLECTED WRITINGS, VOL. 17
PRINCETON: PRINCETON UNIVERSITY PRESS, 1954

The Meaning and Significance of Dreams
BOSTON: SIGO PRESS, 1991

The Myth of the Divine Child
IN: ESSAYS ON A SCIENCE OF MYTHOLOGY
PRINCETON, N.J.: PRINCETON UNIVERSITY PRESS BOLLINGEN
SERIES XXII, 1969. (WITH KARL KERENYI)

Two Essays on Analytical Psychology
COLLECTED WRITINGS, VOL. 7
PRINCETON: PRINCETON UNIVERSITY PRESS, 1972
FIRST PUBLISHED BY ROUTLEDGE & KEGAN PAUL, LTD., 1953

KLEIN, MELANIE

Love, Guilt and Reparation, and Other Works 1921-1945
NEW YORK: FREE PRESS, 1984
(REISSUE EDITION)

Envy and Gratitude and Other Works 1946-1963
NEW YORK: FREE PRESS, 2002
(REISSUE EDITION)

KOESTLER, ARTHUR

The Act of Creation
NEW YORK: PENGUIN ARKANA, 1989.
ORIGINALLY PUBLISHED IN 1964

KRISHNAMURTI, J.

Freedom From The Known
SAN FRANCISCO: HARPER & ROW, 1969

The First and Last Freedom
SAN FRANCISCO: HARPER & ROW, 1975

Education and the Significance of Life
LONDON: VICTOR GOLLANCZ, 1978

BIBLIOGRAPHY

Commentaries on Living
FIRST SERIES
LONDON: VICTOR GOLLANCZ, 1985

Commentaries on Living
SECOND SERIES
LONDON: VICTOR GOLLANCZ, 1986

Krishnamurti's Journal
LONDON: VICTOR GOLLANCZ, 1987

Krishnamurti's Notebook
LONDON: VICTOR GOLLANCZ, 1986

Beyond Violence
LONDON: VICTOR GOLLANCZ, 1985

Beginnings of Learning
NEW YORK: PENGUIN, 1986

The Penguin Krishnamurti Reader
NEW YORK: PENGUIN, 1987

On God
SAN FRANCISCO: HARPER & ROW, 1992

On Fear
SAN FRANCISCO: HARPER & ROW, 1995

The Essential Krishnamurti
SAN FRANCISCO: HARPER & ROW, 1996

The Ending of Time
WITH DR. DAVID BOHM
SAN FRANCISCO: HARPER & ROW, 1985

LAING, RONALD DAVID

Divided Self
NEW YORK: VIKING PRESS, 1991

R.D. Laing and the Paths of Anti-Psychiatry
ED., BY Z. KOTOWICZ
LONDON: ROUTLEDGE, 1997

The Politics of Experience
NEW YORK: PANTHEON, 1983

LIEDLOFF, JEAN

Continuum Concept
IN SEARCH OF HAPPINESS LOST
NEW YORK: PERSEUS BOOKS, 1986
FIRST PUBLISHED IN 1977

LOWEN, ALEXANDER

Bioenergetics
NEW YORK: COWARD, MCGOEGHAM 1975

Depression and the Body
THE BIOLOGICAL BASIS OF FAITH AND REALITY
NEW YORK: PENGUIN, 1992

Fear of Life
NEW YORK: BIOENERGETIC PRESS, 2003

Honoring the Body
THE AUTOBIOGRAPHY OF ALEXANDER LOWEN
NEW YORK: BIOENERGETIC PRESS, 2004

Joy
THE SURRENDER TO THE BODY AND TO LIFE
NEW YORK: PENGUIN, 1995

Love and Orgasm
NEW YORK: MACMILLAN, 1965

Love, Sex and Your Heart
NEW YORK: BIOENERGETICS PRESS, 2004

Narcissism: Denial of the True Self
NEW YORK: MACMILLAN, COLLIER BOOKS, 1983

Pleasure: A Creative Approach to Life
NEW YORK: BIOENERGETICS PRESS, 2004
FIRST PUBLISHED IN 1970

The Language of the Body
PHYSICAL DYNAMICS OF CHARACTER STRUCTURE
NEW YORK: BIOENERGETICS PRESS, 2006

MILLER, ALICE

Four Your Own Good
HIDDEN CRUELTY IN CHILD-REARING AND THE ROOTS OF VIOLENCE
NEW YORK: FARRAR, STRAUS & GIROUX, 1983

Pictures of a Childhood
NEW YORK: FARRAR, STRAUS & GIROUX, 1986

The Drama of the Gifted Child
IN SEARCH FOR THE TRUE SELF
TRANSLATED BY RUTH WARD
NEW YORK: BASIC BOOKS, 1996

Thou Shalt Not Be Aware
SOCIETY'S BETRAYAL OF THE CHILD
NEW YORK: NOONDAY, 1998

The Political Consequences of Child Abuse
IN: THE JOURNAL OF PSYCHOHISTORY 26, 2 (FALL 1998)

MOORE, THOMAS

Care of the Soul
A GUIDE FOR CULTIVATING DEPTH AND SACREDNESS IN EVERYDAY LIFE
NEW YORK: HARPER & COLLINS, 1994

REICH, WILHELM

Children of the Future
ON THE PREVENTION OF SEXUAL PATHOLOGY
NEW YORK: FARRAR, STRAUS & GIROUX, 1983
FIRST PUBLISHED IN 1950

CORE (Cosmic Orgone Engineering)
PART I, SPACE SHIPS, DOR AND DROUGHT
©1984, ORGONE INSTITUTE PRESS
XEROX COPY FROM THE WILHELM REICH MUSEUM

Early Writings 1
NEW YORK: FARRAR, STRAUS & GIROUX, 1975

Ether, God & Devil & Cosmic Superimposition
NEW YORK: FARRAR, STRAUS & GIROUX, 1972
ORIGINALLY PUBLISHED IN 1949

Genitality in the Theory and Therapy of Neurosis
©1980 BY MARY BOYD HIGGINS AS DIRECTOR OF THE WILHELM REICH INFANT
TRUST

People in Trouble
©1974 BY MARY BOYD HIGGINS AS DIRECTOR OF THE WILHELM REICH INFANT
TRUST

BIBLIOGRAPHY

Record of a Friendship
THE CORRESPONDENCE OF WILHELM REICH AND A. S. NEILL
NEW YORK, FARRAR, STRAUS & GIROUX, 1981

Selected Writings
AN INTRODUCTION TO ORGONOMY
NEW YORK: FARRAR, STRAUS & GIROUX, 1973

The Bioelectrical Investigation of Sexuality and Anxiety
NEW YORK: FARRAR, STRAUS & GIROUX, 1983
ORIGINALLY PUBLISHED IN 1935

The Bion Experiments
REPRINTED IN *SELECTED WRITINGS*
NEW YORK: FARRAR, STRAUS & GIROUX, 1973

The Function of the Orgasm (The Orgone, Vol. 1)
ORGONE INSTITUTE PRESS, NEW YORK, 1942

The Cancer Biopathy (The Orgone, Vol. 2)
NEW YORK: FARRAR, STRAUS & GIROUX, 1973

The Invasion of Compulsory Sex Morality
NEW YORK: FARRAR, STRAUS & GIROUX, 1971
ORIGINALLY PUBLISHED IN 1932

The Leukemia Problem: Approach
©1951, ORGONE INSTITUTE PRESS
COPYRIGHT RENEWED 1979
XEROX COPY FROM THE WILHELM REICH MUSEUM

The Mass Psychology of Fascism
NEW YORK: FARRAR, STRAUS & GIROUX, 1970
ORIGINALLY PUBLISHED IN 1933

The Orgone Energy Accumulator
ITS SCIENTIFIC AND MEDICAL USE
©1951, 1979, ORGONE INSTITUTE PRESS
XEROX COPY FROM THE WILHELM REICH MUSEUM

The Schizophrenic Split
©1945, 1949, 1972 BY MARY BOYD HIGGINS AS DIRECTOR OF THE
WILHELM REICH INFANT TRUST
XEROX COPY FROM THE WILHELM REICH MUSEUM

The Sexual Revolution
©1945, 1962 BY MARY BOYD HIGGINS AS DIRECTOR OF THE WILHELM REICH
INFANT TRUST

REID, DANIEL P.

The Tao of Health, Sex & Longevity
A MODERN PRACTICAL GUIDE TO THE ANCIENT WAY
NEW YORK: SIMON & SCHUSTER, 1989

Guarding the Three Treasures
THE CHINESE WAY OF HEALTH
NEW YORK: SIMON & SCHUSTER, 1993

ROSEN, SYDNEY (ED.)

My Voice Will Go With You
THE TEACHING TALES OF MILTON H. ERICKSON
NEW YORK: NORTON & CO., 1991

STEIN, ROBERT M.

Redeeming the Inner Child in Marriage and Therapy
IN: RECLAIMING THE INNER CHILD
ED. BY JEREMIAH ABRAMS
NEW YORK: TARCHER/PUTNAM, 1990, 261 FF.

Steiner, Rudolf

Theosophy
An Introduction to the Spiritual Processes in Human Life
and in the Cosmos
New York: Anthroposophic Press, 1994

Stone, Hal & Stone, Sidra

Embracing Our Selves
The Voice Dialogue Manual
San Rafael, CA: New World Library, 1989

Szasz, Thomas

The Myth of Mental Illness
New York: Harper & Row, 1984

Tart, Charles T.

Altered States of Consciousness
A Book of Readings
Hoboken, N.J.: Wiley & Sons, 1969

What the Bleep Do We Know!?

See Arntz, William

WHITFIELD, CHARLES L.

Healing the Child Within
DEERFIELD BEACH, FL: HEALTH COMMUNICATIONS, 1987

PERSONAL NOTES